LEARNING TO BE A FAMILY

KEN & FLOY SMITH

GREAT COMMISSION PUBLICATIONS

7401 OLD YORK ROAD, PHILADELPHIA, PENNSYLVANIA 19126

Publication of this book has been made possible in part
by a gift from Knox Orthodox Presbyterian Church
in memory of Alice Van Leuven.

ISBN 0-934688-16-8

Printed in USA

Published by Great Commission Publications
7401 Old York Road, Philadelphia, Pennsylvania 19126

TABLE OF CONTENTS

PREFACE

Life in the twentieth century, abounding with new technology, has produced a "how-to" generation. Couple this with traditions rooted in a pioneer spirit and you have some idea of what has come to be known as the American Way of Life.

Somewhere along the line, however, we have lost the *"why*-to" of things. Consequently the motivation for life has suffered. Disappearing are the fundamental reasons which prompt persons to do things: not because they *can* but because they *should*.

Family life is like that. Learning to be a family involves certain methods, but they often vary with personalities. But *why* the family should do certain things—and then learning to do them—determines character and produces discipline.

Christians have a marvelous opportunity, as well as a serious responsibility, to help twentieth-century families recapture the joy of family life's fundamental reason for everything. That reason is simply — God. We are to do everything for God.

This study, therefore, should be understood from that perspective. Learning here will focus on the why of things, for that leads to a life of obedience to God. It also leads to proper relationships. This is true because God has established his purposes for every relationship; and when they are obeyed, he blesses. It's as simple as that. But don't be deceived. Learning that kind of obedience takes time and effort . . . and God's grace.

The study focuses on the family as a whole, not on particular roles. Persons wanting to give attention to personal relationships would do well to consider studying our *Learning to be a Man* or *Learning to be a Woman*, published by Inter-Varsity Press. In those studies we have analyzed the components of a life of maturity. Here we are concerned to see the family, as a unit, develop into full stature.

Twentieth-century families do not need to come apart at the seams. But a house divided against itself cannot stand. United in obedience to Christ, many families of our era are finding lasting peace and prosperity. It is our prayer that this study will afford that kind of hope for all who use it.

Ken and Floy Smith

SECTION ONE

INTRODUCTION

1

A LOOK AT A HAPPY FAMILY

MOD'EL, n. a person or thing
considered as a standard of ex-
cellence to be imitated. (Web-
ster's New 20th Century Dictionary)

"Just hold it by the handle, son, and you'll get the feel of it."

"Like this?"

"Here, let me show you."

"O, I understand. Hey, it's fun!"

Whether learning to mow the lawn, paint a picture, or drive a car, persons get the hang of it by watching someone else. Then they imitate. They learn from the "model."

It is the intent of this book to set before you a model family as God has shown it to us in the Bible. Just by taking a serious look at God's ideal, we have already begun the learning process; hence we have entitled this book *Learning to Be a Family*. A family lifestyle, after all, develops through time and experience as habits are learned. Having a good model will therefore test our habits and practices; and, like any serious Bible study, this one also may require unlearning some things. But still we learn.

Many persons fail to realize that family life can be fun. This does not suggest marriage and the children can be abandoned if the fun wears thin—there's too much of this already in our pursuit-of-happiness society. Our twentieth-century homes desperately need to rediscover a tangible model, a family to be imitated. Young couples today seriously weigh whether there exists any real purpose or permanence in marriage. They search for the answer, and what they see makes them cynical. Our true model must be superior to that.

And it is. We turn to the word of God and Psalm 128. Here God has put on display for a discouraged people a family model, and it's portrayed in song. To know there can be such a family makes one sing.

Now read slowly Psalm 128.

What expressions do you find in these verses conveying the idea of well-being or enjoyment?

_____

_____

Does this sound too good to be true? In the same way Jesus often excited new hope, as for example when he talked to the Samaritan woman who had tried five husbands. Psalm 128 affirms that family life can be deeply rewarding. Why is such a hope important?

_____

_____

_____

_____

Most important to any hope are the grounds on which it rests. As you look at verses 1 and 4, how would you state the underlying principle which makes the possibility of such a family believable?

_____

_____

How does this same root principle show itself in Psalm 127:1?

_____

_____

What additional dimension is added?_____

Take a moment now to reflect on your own family. How would you rate your situation in relation to these principles?

☐ solid   ☐ growing   ☐ shaky   ☐ it's a new idea

In learning to be a family such as Psalm 128 describes we must recognize at the outset that it involves God. Furthermore it involves a commitment to a lifestyle described here as "walking in his way." That's a very simple idea, but it makes the difference. Building on this foundation, our model grows into something wonderful and satisfying. And the simple reason is that it is not

11

"the house that Jack (or Jane, or money, or shrewdness) built."
God does it.

For example, the first four verses state certain propositions which God himself brings into reality. In verses 3 and 4 the wife and children are described. Meditating a bit on the imagery used here, what would you interpret this to say about the woman of the house? The children?

It may seem strange that a man's work looms so important in verse 2, but the work aspect of family life has much to do with family prosperity. While the relationship of work to prosperity seems obvious, how would you expect to see God's blessing on one's work? Can you name four evidences of such blessing?

(1)_____

(2)_____

(3)_____

(4)_____

Family Unity

One characteristic of our model family which impresses a twentieth-century viewer is its togetherness. Ever since the creation of the world God's plan for the family has called for just such a closely-knit relationship between husband and wife, so it should not be a surprise when it spills over into the children's attitudes. How is "God's way" stated in Genesis 2:24?

_____

_____

_____

_____

How did Jesus confirm this principle in his dialog on the matter in Matthew 19:3–8? (Note particularly verse 6.)

_____

_____

_____

_____

Our model, built on Jesus' way, does not appear to be as fragile as one might think. In fact, it has a label stuck on it spelling out its quality: "Unbreakable." Children quickly learn this. To children growing up in an environment which breathes of such unity there emerges a sense of security and rest. Why do you suppose our society has tried to define security in material terms rather than personal commitment?

_____

_____

_____

_____

(A study of Psalm 128 in the Hebrew language reveals the word "blessed" in verse 1 to be the same as "happy" in verse 2. They both derive from a root word meaning "straight" or "right." The word is "Asher," the name that Jacob gave to one of his sons. Would you agree with the inference that children's happiness is not to be essentially a feeling but rather a knowledge that things in their family are based on "right?")

There are many threats to family solidarity. Perhaps that's the reason our song turns from propositional statements to a benediction, beginning with verse 5. If you are not able to define "benediction" look it up in a dictionary.

The term "bless" in verse 5 refers to "good." What is the source of such good?

_____

_____

Perhaps this seems obvious, but how does Psalm 25:8 throw light on it?

_____

_____

Lest we get the impression that blessings come to our model family on a "hot line" from heaven, the psalm indicates that the channel involves "Zion," better described as the city of Jerusalem. For our purposes this means God's people as a whole, or what we might call God's "community." What name do we usually give a community of God's people today?

_____

This interrelatedness with a larger "family" not only lends support to solidarity but also speaks comfort to persons whose families have been fractured by such things as death, separation because of the gospel, or divorce. Draw a circle around the passage below which you believe best portrays this truth.

Galatians 3:27, 28   1 Corinthians 6:9–11   Mark 9:33–37

Our model also includes "grandchildren." Instead of devising ways to keep from having children or get rid of useless old people, the poet speaks of looking forward to what has come to be called the "extended family," or "relatives." Why do so many people think that to apply Genesis 2:24 you must get away from your in-laws and relatives?

_____

_____

The final benediction calls for peace upon God's people, which among other things reminds us that our model family does not live in Utopia but within striking range of enemies. What do you consider to be three major threats to the peace of your family?

(1)_____

(2)_____

(3)_____

What does the apostle Paul say about peace in Romans 5:17ff.?

_____

_____

Having peace with God—that is, legal peace—we can then confront every problem with confidence. According to Philippians 4:6, 7, how can we maintain this quiet assurance?

_____

_____

Summary

To imitate the model family of Psalm 128 we must learn to walk in God's way for the family. This way results because of the activity of God within our family, not because we have adopted a new "do-it-yourself" program. It has unity within itself, but relates both to the larger family of relatives and to the family of God's people, the church.

This study therefore approaches the family as a unit, as God designed it to be. The following chapters will lay the foundation of that unity and then show the practical outcome. To get into this study we must begin to think "family."

Walking in His Ways

1. Is your family at peace with God? What evidence do you have that as a family you are committed to Jesus Christ?
   ☐ We committed our family to obey Christ in 19_____ .
   ☐ We are active members as a family in Christ's church.

☐ We practice family worship on a daily basis.
☐ We don't have much evidence, but we'd like to.
☐ We need particular help as a family at this point.
☐ Other _____

2. As you have viewed this model, have you been made aware of a particular quality God is calling your family to imitate? How? When?

_____

_____

FOUNDATIONS OF FAMILY UNITY

"If the foundations are destroyed, what can the righteous do?" David's enemies were cynically telling him: he'd had it. But instead of panic, peace characterizes his response. Read it for yourself in Psalm 11. A family built on God's foundations can withstand the pressures and maintain peace.

Twentieth-century families, however, have been crumbling. Included in that collapse are scores of husbands, wives and children who profess to believe in Christ. The whole social order is feeling the crunch. Even some churches change their standards to try to adapt to a "right-of-choice" mentality.

God's foundations have not moved, however—we have. And that's the simple reason for the collapse. God has seen to it that other building blocks buckle. He is God, remember! He is not mocked.

Our approach to the family therefore demands a rediscovery of the foundations which keep the family together and prospering. This section introduces us to the solid and heavy foundation stones God laid when he instituted that first family in Eden. To learn to be a family we must have the right foundation.

We have a friend whose company designs foundations for all kinds of structures. After studying the soil in Seattle a few years ago, he drew up the specifications for the foundation of the towering Space Needle. Today the Space Needle is still there—even after earthquakes.

2

UNITY IN FAMILY ORIGIN

"Who made you?"

"God."

"Of what were you made?"

"Of dust."

"What doth that teach you?"

"To be humble and mindful of death."

So former generations sat in their homes and reviewed their catechism. Catechisms, such as the one Martin Luther drew up, were small manuals designed to teach biblical truth by means of questions and answers. Christian families would take time to instruct one another by memorizing the answers.

What made these exercises so valuable, in addition to the time spent together as a family, centered on the fact that the children learned that questions do have answers. Right answers.

Questions are still with us in our modern era but children hear little of right answers, especially from their parents. Our society has been conditioned to believe (and it *is* a "belief") that there can be no definite answers which can be called right. This way of thinking bears the name "relativism." It produces a kind of mentality that can only ask the questions. The result of it all has been the spawning of a generation with college degrees but few answers about fundamental things. This kind of thinking denies the truth which God has given us in the Bible. To be sure, the part most frequently discredited happens to be the part most necessary to find the answers. We mean Genesis, the book of beginnings or origins. We must therefore return to that part of God's word if we want to know "Who made you?" or "Who made the family?". And we will begin at the beginning.

Now thoughtfully read Genesis chapters 1, 2 and 3.

According to this record, written as history, everything we can see, everything there is, has something in common with everything else, giving everything unity. What is that something, particularly evident in Genesis 1:1, 31?

_____

_____

This identity with the living God, the Creator, should not be confused with pantheism, which claims that everything *is* God. This viewpoint forbids there being a living God who can be known personally. In contrast, how were God's people, according to Deuteronomy 6:4, 5,

(1) to understand God?_____

(2) to treat God?_____

This living or "being" attribute of God, and hence his know-ableness, can be found throughout the Bible. But it becomes

22

very explicit in his name YAHWEH (or JEHOVAH). So that we can keep this name in mind as we read the Bible, translators have used the word LORD in capital letters. The term itself derives from the verb "to be," so God called himself YAHWEH or "I AM" when talking to Moses in Exodus 3:14. How did Jesus refer to this term in John 8:58? (Compare this with John 10:30.)

_____

_____

Here is a marvelous mystery. While the Bible teaches that God is *one*, it also teaches that more than one person comprise the godhead. How does this truth appear in Matthew 28:19?

_____

_____

Keeping in mind, then, this doctrine of God's nature called by the term "Trinity," let's go back again to Genesis. Why does 1:26 say "Let *us* make man . . .?"

_____

_____

This way of talking about God, the Three in One, must be accepted as truth. In spite of the way some disbelieve and try to ridicule it, the idea permeates creation. Take the term "universe," for example, so common in our conversation. With so many parts to creation, we talk about it as a whole and we give it a term spelling unity. However, because so much of our modern education has come to treat the Bible and its teaching about God as irrelevant to learning, the unity which at one time gave integrity or wholeness to knowledge has of necessity been lost. So today, when talking about something as practical as family life, the very *idea* of unity has lost its meaning. In short, the foundation has been removed. According to Romans 1:21, what is the inevitable result of refusing to acknowledge God?

Why? (See Gen. 1:28.)

Notice how this idea of unity in God's nature carries over into man's makeup. While many ponder "Who am I?", the Bible answers the question, and simply enough for a child to see. "And God created man. . . ." What distinguishes God's creative activity from man's? (You may wish to read Hebrews 11:3 before you answer.)

Getting to the root of the matter, why is it important for us to come to terms with this truth of God's having *created* man?

Note the phrase, repeated three times in Genesis 1:26, 27, identifying the pattern God used for making man. What does that term suggest about man in

Genesis 9:5, 6? _____

_____

Ephesians 4:22–24? _____

_____

Man therefore has a unique identity in relation to his Creator, and we will explore this more in later chapters. However, in Genesis 1:27 what additional and very significant aspect of man is introduced?

_____

_____

Did you notice how the Bible uses the term "man" in a collective or generic sense? It is proper to speak of "man" and mean both sexes in the same way we can speak of God and mean all three persons. How does Genesis 2:22, 23 further underscore this unity in man?

_____

_____

We must pursue this even more. Without yet delving into God's purpose for man and hence his purpose for the family, we must recognize the absolute necessity of both sexes for there to be a family. How does the biological design of the sexes alone prove this unity?

_____

_____

Our point here in no way suggests that because someone remains single there must be something wrong with him or her. It is fundamental to Scripture that one's sex cannot be understood or appreciated without accepting it as God's creation in the first place, and then accepting it as the counterpart to the opposite sex in the second place. How could Psalm 139:13–16 help parents explain these things to their children?

_____

_____

_____

_____

In sharp contrast, any society disregarding God's record of the creation of man will soon lose its way in preserving any unity for marriage, family, or even society. What ultimatum did Jesus pronounce on this principle in Matthew 19:6?

_____

_____

_____

_____

We must also add that God's word gives no indication whatsoever that a person could be *born* a homosexual or lesbian. Instead the Bible simply asserts our capability to reproduce as proof that we are, and therefore are to be, male *or* female. (Children born with deformity of their sex organs should not be called homosexual or lesbian when precise medical terms can be used.) Denial of one's sex, or rejection of the opposite sex, must be explained as a denial of God's order of things. Such denial is a learned behavior, conscious or unconscious. And it is encouraging that by the grace of God and with supportive help, it can be unlearned. Note 1 Corinthians 6:9–11. What is the significance of the expression "And such were some of you . . ."?

_____

_____

_____

_____

How then does this recognition of the origin of man, male and female, help to explain the meaning of "one flesh" in Genesis 2:24?

_____

_____

Summary

According to God's word, behind every family there exists a unity built in from creation. As God made man like himself, so man was designed to reflect God's image. And man must do this *as man,* male and female. Sex can therefore be understood, accepted, appreciated and enjoyed by taking God's word for it. With an understanding of the true origin of man and the family, our unbreakable model of Psalm 128 can begin to have credibility. To be sure, sin has distorted the picture, but sin has *not* altered these truths. In trying to clear up the distortions, we build on God's truth.

Walking in His Ways

1. Would you agree or disagree that for a person to love his or her married partner means fundamentally to treat that person as God's creation with a God-given sex?

   _____

2. As a result of studying this chapter, do you believe it is reasonable to call a presiding female a "chairperson" instead of a "chairman?" Explain why.

   _____

   _____

3. Over and over again our modern way of life as a society denies the underlying truths of Genesis 1–3. Can you identify such denial in a current

   TV program?   _____

   movie?   _____

   book?   _____

   magazine?   _____

UNITY IN FAMILY ORIGIN

4. If you have children have you explained to them in simpli-
   fied terms their origin and sexuality in terms of Genesis 1? If
   not, could you now? If so, will you?

_____

_____

3

UNITY IN FAMILY PURPOSE

Do you, John, take Mary whose hand you hold in yours, to be your lawfully wedded wife, and do you promise before _____ and in the presence of these witnesses that you will be to her a true, a faithful, and a loving husband as long as you both shall _____ ?

Until recently there would be little question about what words should fill these blanks in the marriage vow. Today these words are being changed, an indication that twentieth-century man is adopting a new purpose for marriage and the family.

Before we analyze this new perspective let's pause long enough to establish two truths in the Bible having to do with the duration of marriage.

According to Romans 7:1–3, where marriage appears as an illustration of another truth, how long are marriage vows binding?

_____

_____

How do Jesus' words about marriage in Luke 20:27–36 (see

31

the context, too) place time limits on the husband-and-wife relationship?

_____

_____

The Bible therefore speaks very plainly about how long marriage is, and is not, to last. Such instructions prove very helpful. They set plain boundaries on the marriage institution. That is the reason why the last word in the traditional vow has read "as long as we both shall _live_," not _"love."_ Because God himself established this blessed relationship and set these boundaries, the first blank in our vow has normally read "God." What is your understanding of this vow? Or any vow?

_____

_____

_____

_____

It makes sense then that if God created man male and female he also had the right and the wisdom to pronounce his purpose for marriage. Again we return to Genesis 1 and look for "his way" so we can walk in it like our model in Psalm 128.

According to Genesis 1:26–28, what was God's reason for creating man? (And don't forget: man here means male and female.)

_____

_____

_____

_____

As you think over these truths deeply rooted in God's word you should be aware that the book of Genesis—especially these early chapters—condenses what could have filled a library. God chose not to include many details that beckon our curiosity about "the beginning," but he has told us what is necessary to live and walk in his way. Many persons who study Genesis lose sight of the very significant doctrinal teaching made plain here, which commands our belief and obedience. For example, the fact of creation alone teaches us who we are and to whom we and everything that was made belong. This relationship between God and his creation the Bible terms a "covenant" relationship.

The matters raised in Genesis 1–3 are indeed foundational, not only for the family but for a proper perspective on all reality, seen and unseen. Our society has to a very large extent been educated to think these chapters are mythical instead of historical. Consequently, when they want to get hard facts about things they take the scientific method as their point of reference, unaware that this method has come to mean man's faith in man. Today's generation has not rejected Genesis (as the former generation did) but has seldom if ever _heard_ Genesis, not to mention having it credibly explained. In what way does Matthew 7:24–28 explain why so many homes are falling apart?

_____

_____

_____

_____

Returning to God's purpose for the family, we can recognize
Genesis 1 as a summation of creation where man can also find a
clear answer to "Why am I here?". Using Genesis 1:26–28, how
could you explain to your children why they are here?

_____

_____

_____

_____

Genesis 2 spells out some details. In the order of creation who
was made first, Adam or Eve? (See also 1 Timothy 2:13.)

_____

_____

If you were to use one word to size up Adam as he is pictured
in Genesis 2:18–20, what word would it be?

_____

What term does the Bible use for woman in both Genesis 2:18
and 2:20?

_____

_____

It is evident from Genesis 1:28 and 2:8 that the family as an institution (that is, something established—in this case by God) shares one purpose under the Creator. Both husband and wife, with their children, participate in that mission. Check below what you believe Adam's response might have been when he first saw Eve as recorded in Genesis 2:22, 23.

☐ Aha—I've finally found someone to do my washing!
☐ Perfect—now our corporation can produce and begin to make a profit!
☐ What a slick chick—she'll make my day!
☐ A companion at last—we can serve God together!

While marriage has its own particular purpose from God, at the same time this happy relationship between Adam and Eve (see 2:25 where they were without shame) pictured man's relationship with God. Here in a word we see an integration of love and responsibility. As man saw himself as God's creation and at the same time enjoyed God as his friend, so in the marriage covenant Adam and Eve found their unity in purpose to be a happy mandate. How does Genesis 1:28 show God's design in this integration? (You may want to refer to Psalm 128:1 again.)

_____

_____

Even a quick reading now of Genesis 3 will reveal historically how and why this happiness evaporated. Substituting his own way for God's—the essence of sin, by the way—Adam broke covenant and brought upon himself, his family, the human race and even the very ground God's disfavor and curse. Would you say on the basis of Genesis 2:16, 17 that Adam had an excuse? Explain.

_____

_____

_____

_____

How did God's curse affect his original purpose for man and the family according to Genesis 3:14–19? Check one.
- ☐ God's original purpose was abolished.
- ☐ The purpose remained but mankind would have to struggle to achieve it.
- ☐ The purpose remained but God alone could remove the difficulties and enable him to achieve it.

We have thus in sobering words an explanation for two aspects of family life:
(1) the reason why family life has become painful and disappointing, and
(2) the basis on which a family can rebuild with the purpose and blessing of God.

Does your family know why people experience physical death?

This basis for rebuilding appears in Genesis 3:15 where God promises in graphic language how "the seed of the woman" would crush Satan, the villain in this historical episode. Who was the "seed of the woman?" (Hint: 1 John 3:8)

_____

_____

How good it is to know that God has provided a way by which he restores man and delivers him from the curse of his sin. That way must be understood and adopted in order to walk in it. So when our model family of Psalm 128 walks in God's way we understand they are committed to the seed of the woman. So even in the Old Testament, family life had to be built on the foundation of God's grace in Christ! Is that a new idea to you? How does John 14:6 relate to these things?

_____

_____

_____

_____

This gracious way for restoration represents another means by which God relates to his people, the old covenant having been broken. It is very important for our society to face up to this different covenant, for it is not a do-it-yourself proposition. Instead it has been called "the covenant of grace." How does Ephesians 2:8, 9 explain this?

_____

_____

_____

_____

Another slant on this covenant stands out in the nature of the marriage relationship itself. See Ephesians 5:22–23, a passage often read at Christian weddings. What point is Paul making here?

_____

_____

_____

_____

Summary

Every family has a dual purpose. First, the family stands as a symbol of Christ's covenant with his bride, his church. This in itself gives every household walking in his way a significant purpose. Together as a unity they portray the glory of God's love for his people in Christ. And in the same way Christ keeps covenant with his bride (he won't divorce his people), so the fidelity of the family bond signals hope for a broken world. And of course the children are the first to pick up that signal.

Second, with the grace of Christ now as its resource to overcome sin and its curse, the family as a unity picks up on God's original assignment in Genesis 1:26–28. Life as a covenant bond with God gives a coherence, a meaning and a motivation to man for every responsibility. Genesis 2:24 then means that as one flesh Adam and Eve enjoy and serve God and each other. What a wonderful environment for children.

Walking in His Ways

1. In the light of this study, do you think the trend toward a wife's having to have her own career for fulfillment is good?

   _____

2. Do you, like many people today, feel uncomfortable using the term "helper" as Genesis 2:18, 20 uses it? Why or why not?

   _____

   _____

3. How would you rate your family in unity of purpose? Using number one as very poor and five as very good, give your family its proper figure. How would this compare with last year's rating?

   _____

   _____

4. Here's a project: Sit down as a family, pass out slips of paper to those old enough to participate and ask everyone to write down what he thinks your family purpose is (not what it ought to be). Compare your impressions. Do they reflect the two-sided purpose in this chapter's summary?

4

UNITY IN FAMILY STRUCTURE

"Dad, may I have the car tonight?"

"Did you ask your mother?"

"Yeah."

"What did she say?"

"No!"

"Well, why are you asking me then?"

Lines of communication and authority go hand in hand, and children are to learn this in the home. What would you say a teenager is taught about family structure in the above interchange?

_____

_____

What does it show that he has already learned from the fact that he asked?

_____

_____

Learning to be a family comes almost naturally when we follow the Designer's blueprint. Twentieth-century man, however, has a way of rejecting God's way. Consequently our families fail to understand or regard loving authority at home. Children from such homes reproduce the problem when they get married, and the spiral continues its descent. Let's see how this breakdown began in history.

If you skim over Genesis 4 and the tragedy that took place in the first family between Cain and Abel you come to one of Cain's descendants named Lamech (see verse 19). What new twist in family structure emerges here?

_____

_____

While it must be acknowledged that God tolerated this innovation in the Old Testament, he never commanded it. How would you interpret God's desire in the matter from the following Scripture references?

Genesis 2:24_____

Exodus 20:14, 17_____

Matthew 19:3–8 _____

For that matter, how many wives are mentioned in our model family of Psalm 128?

People are often confused about the polygamy in the Old Testament. While many men had more than one wife no instance is recorded when a woman had more than one husband.

However, the New Testament shows clearly that when Christ came he reaffirmed to God's covenant community the creation structure for marriage: one man and one woman. This unity in structure can be seen in 1 Timothy 3:1, 2 and 3:12. How?

_____

_____

_____

_____

But there's more. Since the family is made up of more than one person, we can liken it to a team with a single purpose but with differing positions for each member to play. In a society that likes to throw away the rule book it's no wonder the game loses its luster. Have you ever heard of a football game where there were eleven quarterbacks on each side? Even children recognize the foolishness of pretending there's no significant difference between dad and mom in the family. Review for a moment how God has constructed us physically. The structure of the woman's body requires women to bear children if children are to be born. Why do an increasing number of women complain about this unfortunate circumstance?

_____

_____

_____

_____

Do you think they are serious in their complaint?

Take another obvious instance: What is needed if babies are to live and grow?

_____

_____

These self-evident factors in God's creation when accepted as from God can mean great enjoyment and success. Man's problem is not his structure—it's his attitude. It's his rejection of the doctrine God has instilled in his very nature. The problem resides deep in his rebellious spirit. If you wish to pursue this, review Romans 1:18–32. What is the reason given in verse 28 why people do things which are improper?

_____

_____

_____

_____

We must be careful not to be deceived by some who teach by subtle persuasion that God's word leaves family relationships and structure up to each culture to work out as it chooses. To deny God's order of family structure for any cause is to court chaos. It is to deny God of his honor and the family of its blessedness. Are you conscious of those influences coming into your family? Can you put the following general influences in their order of impact on you and yours?

☐ TV drama	☐ TV newscasts
☐ Radio music	☐ Radio talk shows
☐ Movies	☐ Graphic arts
☐ Advertisements	☐ Music recordings
☐ School courses	☐ Divorce statistics
☐ Abortion laws	☐ Newspaper comics
☐ Porno magazines	☐ Clean magazines
☐ Clothing styles	☐ Hair styles

An important factor in considering family organization as the Bible gives it to us has to do with attitude in general. What does Christ both demonstrate and demand in his kingdom? See Mark 10:42–45.

_____

_____

_____

_____

A power-structure mentality has no place in the covenant community in general and in the family in particular. What spirit takes its place in

Ephesians 5:21? _____

1 Peter 3:8, 9? _____

Both of these passages attach to structural guidelines, which shows at the outset that structural patterns are couched in terms of togetherness. This mutual support, sometimes called team spirit (or *esprit de corps*) acts like oil, keeping things running smoothly and quietly.

(Persons who argue that the Christian community functions like a body rather than an organization have used a false antithesis. The human body is one of the most marvelous and intricate demonstrations of organization imaginable.)

Therefore, having stressed the spirit of the whole we now turn to simple, definitive structural roles that God has established for the family. Let's look at Colossians 3:18–21. Describe the role for each of the following:

(1) wife _____

(2) husband _____

(3) children _____

(4) father _____

While many go into great detail about distinctive roles, it remains the view of the authors of this study that the emphasis in the Bible focuses on the family as a unit. The respective roles are important *because* the family is an integral whole. To deny the roles is to deny the unit. But once people have accepted their roles they simply concentrate on how to play as a team. That takes everybody. How do these passages from Genesis stress unity?

Genesis 1:27 _____

Genesis 1:28 _____

Genesis 2:24_____

Let's assume the structure of roles for the family that the Bible describes. In succeeding chapters we will concentrate on how the family functions as a unity or a team. We do not want a collection of stars. Anyone who dominates the family at the expense of any other member tends to destroy what God designed to be balanced and beautiful.

Read the following passages and write a summary statement about the structural unity you see. Read them all before you try to write anything.

John 14:10–26   John 15:23–26   John 16:13–15

_____

_____

_____

_____

Summary

We conclude that when God ordained man and woman to cleave together into one flesh, they were in fact a unity. This unity must be kept pure, because that's God's structural design from creation and from his covenant in Christ. Furthermore, he has given the husband and wife distinct roles which, when combined, demonstrate harmony in fulfilling God's assignment for man. Children from their birth have a role to fulfill as well, which expands but maintains the original wholeness. With a commitment to its God-given structure, the family can learn how to function in unity. It's all wrapped up in learning how to walk in his ways.

Walking in His Ways

1. Some people find their marriage strained because at heart they are still single. How would one develop a proper disposition toward marriage?

   _____

   _____

2. Teamwork involves a lot of give-and-take. Do your family members help each other fulfill their respective roles? What does this give-and-take require?

   _____

   _____

3. Structure without affection can be very cold—even sterile. How would you rate the affection level of your family?

   _____

   _____

4. Have you discussed and worked out your biblical roles as a family? If not, could you?

   _____

   _____

FUNCTIONING WITH FAMILY UNITY

Remember "the birds and the bees"? The origin of this subtle way of talking about sex life and having babies, according to one report, derived from the way children were once taught in school. By understanding the reproductive processes of these other creatures the children were given credit for making the connection about man and woman.

In circles where people recognize the wonder of God's creation they don't have to cloak their talk in terms of the birds and the bees because it's thought to be vulgar to speak plainly. But they do treasure the wonderful way God leads his people when they, like the birds and the bees, obey what he has created to function naturally—and a bit mysteriously.

When we talk about family function we will avoid the tendency to talk technique and look instead at what God wants us to do as family. We want to preserve something of the mystery of learning as God unfolds his will. Life in covenant with him is personal and we learn through the process of obedience, actually walking in his ways. He teaches us how to do this, so we will find ourselves talking about him, not about techniques.

We will consider how the family walks in his ways in four different yet related areas. As the family worships, works, relaxes and ministers, God enables them to understand his plan. So we will leave the birds and the bees and get on with the matter of obedience. This is a big part of learning to be a family.

5

WORSHIP – AN ATMOSPHERE

In a society where unity of purpose fragments and where technology spawns specialization, people do not associate worship with family. Worship is what you do in church.

However, to a family that walks in his ways like the model in Psalm 128, everything exists because of God and *for* God. Romans 11:36 affirms this truth. What are we summoned to do as a result?

This awareness of God seven days a week shows up in Psalm 128 in verse 1 in terms of the "fear of the LORD." For many folks an attitude of fear toward God casts a dark shadow over their idea of a warm relationship with a heavenly Father. Do you agree with this?

The Bible often associates the fear of God with a happy or blessed state. For example, what blessings come to those who fear God in the following passages?

Psalm 31:19 _____

Psalm 33:18, 19 _____

Psalm 34:7, 8 _____

On the other hand, how did Adam act when he heard God coming in Genesis 3:10? Why?

_____

_____

Here we have what appears to be a contradiction. Many portions of Scripture speak of the blessings attached to fearing the Lord, but Adam's fear made him hide from God. Romans 3:18 has something to add about sinful man and the fear of God. What is it?

_____

_____

The problem resolves itself when we recognize that to fear God on the one hand is to take our relationship to him seriously, while *not* to fear him on the other hand is playing with fire. Consequently we expect a rebellious society to talk down and discount as undesirable the fear of the Lord. But having said that, do you think Adam had reason to fear God? Explain.

_____

_____

_____

_____

Do you think our model family in Psalm 128 has reason to fear God? Or your family for that matter—do you have reason?

_____

_____

_____

_____

When we review the events of Genesis 3 we must acknowledge that in Adam all mankind has come under the curse of sin. We live in a cursed universe. However, as Genesis 3:15 foreshadows, the seed of the woman through his own suffering destroyed Satan's power. As passages like Romans 5:1 point out, by putting our faith in the Lord Jesus Christ we are justified (declared righteous) before God and the root cause of our fear, sin and its curse, has been removed.

However, with that new relationship established by faith in Christ we become God's sons and daughters, and he begins to work in us to make us like his Son. Jesus is holy, so this work is called "sanctification." With the fear of eternal punishment removed by justification, we find in its place a loving respect for God such as a child will have for his parents. This deep respect and reverence grows, so it's not strange that children learn more about their relation to God as they relate to their parents. Too often this is terribly distorted, but where there exists a conscious concern to walk in his ways God uses the parent-child relationship to open a youngster's eyes to himself. Let's see how it works out in day-to-day experience. We will consider four fundamental ingredients producing this atmosphere.

The Presence of Sin

Most families need no one to tell them they are not perfect. Problems come in all sizes and colors, but dealing with our sins is the most important. For a start, what does 1 John 1:8 teach us? (According to 1 John 5:13, was John writing to Christians or non-Christians?)

_____

_____

Here's an example: Job had children; how did he anticipate sin problems in his home in Job 1:4, 5?

_____

_____

Outside the home sin and its effects are widespread. How does Paul see the creation in this light in Romans 8:20, 21?

_____

_____

We should not be caught off guard when sin shows itself in our own families, and we should always call it by its right name: sin. When we talk about world problems we can and should identify the root problem: sin. How does this approach in itself introduce a healthy attitude toward God?

_____

_____

_____

_____

The Power of Jesus

The real problem caused by sin, whatever people think, does not essentially reside with man but with God. A social lifestyle that consistently defines our problems in terms of man denies God and hence fails to understand sin. How does this God-related nature of sin show itself in Genesis 3? (Compare this with Genesis 6:5–8.)

_____

_____

_____

_____

In the light of these things, what stands out in Jesus' title in John 1:29?

_____

_____

According to Exodus 12:7-13, where God institutes the rite of the Passover, do you see anything significant about *where* the blood of the lamb was to be sprinkled?

_____

_____

_____

_____

How does that same emphasis exhibit itself in Paul's preaching centuries later in a place called Philippi? Acts 16:31-33 reveals this.

_____

_____

Throughout the Bible God's solution to sin always points us to the sacrifical death of his Son. God himself applies it to the family. There is therefore unity in deliverance from sin, and together the family learns to kneel as sinners before God in the name of Jesus. Thus they learn to worship.

The Place of Forgiveness

According to 1 John 1:9, what happens to our sins when we bow down and confess them? (See also Proverbs 28:13.)

_____

_____

What will happen if we do not turn from our sins? See how Isaiah 59:1, 2 relates to this.

_____

_____

Seeking God's forgiveness affects our interpersonal relations as well. How are we reminded of this every time we pray the Lord's Prayer (Luke 11:4)?

_____

_____

A true recognition of our sins, coupled with an awareness of Jesus' atonement for sin, leads us to true confession and repentance. Forgiveness in Christ begets in us a spirit of forgiveness, which in turn prepares us for the fourth fundamental.

The Purpose of Scripture

Since life is covenantal—that is, to be lived out in relationship to God—we can understand why God gave us the Bible. Someone has said that the word of God is not just information, but communication. When we have experienced his forgiveness in Christ we willingly receive his directions and encouragement. In short, the Bible becomes his will for us.

How did Jesus speak of the "obedient life" in John 8:31, 32?

_____

_____

How did the apostle Paul remind his colleague Timothy about the Scriptures in 2 Timothy 3:14–17? List as many purposes or benefits from God's word as you can from the passage.

_____

_____

_____

_____

If God created the world by his word, if God brings sinners to repentance by his word, does it not follow that God provides the resource for obedience by his word? Does Acts 20:32 say this?

_____

_____

Clearly the Bible has always been central in Christian family life. The family Bible used to be important, and still is—not as a place to record the names of ancestors and grandchildren (though that's not a bad idea) but as a means of grace for the household. God blesses the family through his word.

Summary

Following the lead of our model family, we have concluded that to fear God provides a proper atmosphere in which a family should function. We give this our primary attention; for unless the family understands its true relationship to God, its constant need for the forgiveness God provides in Christ, there can be no basis for a happy and united walk together. The fear of God leads us to true worship, so we have not been looking at worship as just a matter of technique but as a posture of the heart. In learning to be a family we learn to bow down before God, to kneel before him as our holy Father, to take seriously our own sinfulness. Reverence for God and his salvation must *always* undergird our procedures.

Walking in His Ways

1. At one place the Bible says, ". . . by the law is the knowledge of sin." Do you and your children know the Ten Commandments? Have you considered memorizing Exodus 20:1–17 as a family?

_____

2. Talking together as a family provides an atmosphere in itself. Have you talked together about how Christ's death on the cross has affected your lives?

_____

3. Discipline has become a lost art in many homes, largely due to the influence of lawless thinking. Do you base the discipline in your family on the Bible? Do you work with your children concerning obedience to God in specific instances?

_____

4. Some parents feel hurt when their children become involved

in particular sins. They take it as a personal offense. Do you think this is right? What are the alternatives?

_____

_____

6

WORSHIP — IN PRACTICE

> Now I lay me down to sleep;
> I pray Thee, Lord, my soul to keep.
> If I should die before I wake,
> I pray Thee, Lord, my soul to take.

Whether it's the bedtime prayer or folding our hands before we eat, most of us learn to pray at home. But it is also true that persons also learn *not* to pray at home. Example counts! It counted with Jesus and his disciples—look at Luke 11:1. What did the disciples ask Jesus? Why?

_____

_____

What was Jesus' response?

_____

_____

Perhaps you and your children already know this prayer; but have you ever thought it through, petition by petition? Learning to worship God as a family goes beyond memorizing and analyzing prayers, however: it involves learning to live our lives in the power of God. In other words, our motivation and energy are not to come from self-discipline—that's how the Pharisees lived. Rather we are to *live out* our union with Jesus Christ. Since our lives are bound up in Him we must not only come to God through him but also learn to draw upon him for our living. How does each of the following stress this truth?

Ephesians 2:10 _____

Ephesians 3:14–19 _____

Ephesians 6:10 _____

When families take their relationship to God seriously and draw upon Jesus by his Spirit to give them power for obedience, they have reason for practical ways to seek God. Let's explore four ways the family can do this together.

Prayers before Meals and Bedtime

People learn to acknowledge God very quickly when they recognize he has supplied their food. We really don't need to go into specific Scripture to recognize the validity of asking a blessing on, or giving thanks for, our meals. It is evident how walking in his ways produces almost naturally such a practice.

What general rule of life does Paul outline for Christians in 1 Corinthians 10:31?

_____

_____

If Jesus teaches us to pray "Give us this day our daily bread," what logically follows when God answers our petition?

_____

_____

What do you think children (and adults) are learning from _not_ praying before meals as a general practice?

_____

_____

Can you think of any reason why praying before bedtime became another common custom among Christians? (Ponder Psalm 4:8.)

_____

_____

Recognizing that these prayers take only a very little time each day, consider the rewards. What do these prayers mean

(1) to God? _____

(2) to the family? _____

Worshiping with God's People

Next to learning to fold their hands and close their eyes, children learn about worship as the family joins with others on each Lord's day for united worship. When God and not personal comfort is kept at the center of this practice, the family gains beyond measure and the Christian community grows. What do we learn about the Old Testament practice of community worship in Luke 4:16–22?

_____

_____

_____

_____

The New Testament church made some changes in this practice, but maintained some things too. Looking at Acts 20:7 and 1 Corinthians 16:2, what would you say

(1) was different? _____

(2) was the same? _____

It's not strange to find a general trend in our society to tailor the Lord's day and the practice of worship to our own purposes rather than God's. Even Christian families have often been caught up in self-interest and have isolated themselves from being part of a _people_. And yet when we read 2 Corinthians 6:16–18, an Old Testament reference by the way, what term do we discover to identify the church?

_____

_____

According to this passage, what position does God call the church to assume in relation to the world?

_____

_____

What does this position *not* mean (cf. John 17:15)?

_____

_____

Recognizing from this and other passages God's delight in his people—and their delight in him—try to enumerate five blessings God provides for his people as families through their regular assembly for his worship.

(1)_____

(2)_____

(3)_____

(4)_____

(5)_____

What does contact with other Christian families have to do with encouraging Christian marriages? (Did you notice 2 Corinthians 6:14?)

_____

_____

Family Worship

When the poet Robert Burns penned the lines to "The Cotter's Saturday Night" he described with rapt pleasure his memory of a Scottish cottager gathering his family after the evening meal with "Let us worship God." There in humble setting they sang psalms, read the Bible and knelt to pray. Burns then wrote:

From scenes like these old Scotia's grandeur springs,
That makes her lov'd at home, rever'd abroad.

Burns was correct, and the authors of this study agree that nothing a family does as a family means more than daily family worship. To be sure, it does not stand alone but adds that God-centered dimension to total family living which in itself becomes an impregnable defense against evil. Before such a practice can become established there must be a degree of commitment. How did Joshua declare his purpose for his family in Joshua 24:14, 15?

_____

_____

Do you believe family worship meets the requirements of Deuteronomy 6:4–9? In what way?

_____

_____

Look at Psalm 34:1–3. How does family worship relate to the togetherness mentioned here?

_____

_____

(You may want to meditate on the entire psalm, noting verse 11 and what follows.)

Learning to sing to God, listen to God, and talk to God leads a family to God-oriented thinking and habits. On the other hand the neglect of bowing down together leads to unsolved tensions, unconfessed offenses and misplaced values. What do you believe to be the greatest problem in getting started in this practice and how would you meet it?

_____

_____

_____

_____

Private Devotions

With all that has been said about worship one aspect remains: being alone with God. While this may not seem to fit our "together" motif, family life may either foster or frustrate such privacy with God. Like all the rest this too comes into practice most easily through the example of others. What model do we have in Mark 1:35?

_____

_____

Many of the Psalms use the first personal pronoun "I." Take Psalm 138 for example, written by King David. How would you say he feels toward the Lord at this time?

☐ depressed ☐ jubilant ☐ angry ☐ thankful

What words in the psalm do you believe best express David's understanding of God?

_____

_____

When he uses the phrase "what concerns me" (vs. 8) or "his purpose for me," would you associate the meaning with Philippians 1:6? Explain.

_____

_____

_____

_____

Proverbs 4:23 has much to do with family life. When the spirit of Christ is working privately to perfect our weaknesses, the family is affected. The same spirit helps us to respond positively to the weaknesses of one another, rather than to become cynical and tense. Parents who find it difficult to communicate with their children need to seek God's help, learning how he communicates with *his* children. Children who are familiar with their parents' private worship habits will begin to pick these up naturally by example, finding intimate fellowship with God when they are alone. Often conversation will naturally turn to things learned alone with God. So there's reason for the family to work at "keeping their hearts with all diligence."

Summary

The atmosphere of worship must be cultivated, but how? We give ourselves to seek God together in practical and spontaneous ways. Remembering that we have been created and redeemed to serve him, we actually work at ways to show him our love and seek out his strength for joyful obedience. We must not be mechanical about it, but we should work at habit patterns which demonstrate our God-centered commitment. Confronting our daily problems can affect our worship, but more powerfully our worship will affect our problems. Many interpersonal problems will clear up through a simple prayer of confession followed by open conversation. Others may have to be worked out over a period of time, but the routine of daily worship will be blessed by God. His care for us will permeate our own spirits. No wonder our model family finds happiness!

Walking in His Ways

1. Let's evaluate your family and worship. First put a check mark beside your usual practice:
   - ☐ prayers before meals and _____ bedtime;
   - ☐ worship with God's people, the church;
   - ☐ family worship _____ daily _____ occasionally;
   - ☐ private devotions _____ everyone _____ some.

   Now draw a line under any you believe need attention in a particular way at this time. What should you do about each?

   _____

   _____

2. What would you say about the value system of a family that has no time for worship as a family? What are both children and parents learning from this?

_____

_____

3. Can you understand why the family that neglects worship may have to hunt for counsel, books, tapes, and even drugs to try to handle its problems? What real help is needed?

_____

_____

4. Some families believe that getting started in family worship can best be done by attaching it to a regular mealtime, like another dessert. Would you agree? What if the family never eats together?

_____

7

WORK — LIFE WITH RELEVANCE

At the time of the first International Labor and Management Prayer Breakfast held in Pittsburgh in 1978 the president of the United Steel Workers of America was asked by a reporter, "Is this prayer breakfast religious or philosophical?"

The mentality of today's culture can be detected more often through its questions than through its answers. By asking this question the reporter revealed his own bias, and frankly it's the bias of many people. It's the idea that some areas are religious and some are not. To most the area of work would have to be classified as nonreligious. This type of thinking has been taught and learned at home.

In answer to the question "Why work?" twentieth-century man faces three basic life-systems:
(1) to reach a Utopian dream for society,
(2) to realize the goal of self-improvement, and
(3) to seek the kingdom of God.

At first glance only one of these seems religious. But on second thought, what religious perspectives underlie the other two?

_____

_____

_____

When Psalm 128 describes our model family it calls attention to work in the next breath after saying they "walk in his ways." This really makes sense. After all, the greatest amount of time spent in any one activity puts work as number one. It is critical that our perspective on work embrace the logical extension of our walking in his ways and not be based on an inferior foundation. Everything, of course, is "religious"—it's just a question of which religious viewpoint will dominate. People get all tangled up in their views and practices. Read Isaiah 44:6–17: what did God's prophet accuse his people of doing here?

_____   _____

_____

_____

_____

Some people do give themselves religiously to their work. But if they lose sight of work's purpose they will soon be caught up in all kinds of strange and inconsistent customs. Children detect these things when a family claims to be Christian and yet has non-Christian views determining their lifestyle. Work has its roots in our view of God. So once again we must go back to the book of beginnings.

After reading Genesis 1:26–30 how would you define "work"?

_____

_____

Do you see any connection between God's making man "after his image" and "work"? (Is Genesis 2:2, 3 a tip?)

_____

_____

Almost every question a person can ask is both religious and philosophical. One need not have a formal education to realize that our basic perspective on God, life and things necessarily influences how we answer questions. Viewpoints also set our standard of values, which means we must be sure of our perspectives. Our children are interested in these things: have you asked *them* why they think a person should work? What did they say?

_____

_____

_____

_____

Would you say their answer was "religious"? In what way?

_____

_____

As far as Genesis 1:28 is concerned, would you normally include bearing and rearing children as part of God's work assignment for man? (Obviously "man" here means male and female.)

_____

_____

73

How does the modern option of willful abortion fit with this command?

_____

_____

Let's try now to pull some things together. At the outset of creation, God himself worked to bring about all that he made. He then gave man the assignment to populate the earth, then rule and subdue it. Man in this sense is to imitate his Creator, who both worked and rested. If work has become God's assignment to man, to whom is man accountable for his work? Why?

_____

_____

How would you say such "motivation" could affect the various work aspects of a family, for example, in terms of

(1) dad? _____

(2) mom? _____

(3) children? _____

Now go back to page 71 and review your answer(s) to the question about the three twentieth-century systems man faces regarding the reason for work. Taking these life-systems at face value, can you see why working in terms of the kingdom of God is so radically different? Would you agree with the man who said the thing that makes the kingdom of God so important is simply God?

When work has been performed as an extension of "walking

in his ways," according to Psalm 128 how does this affect the family?

_____

_____

Do you think this same effect could also be seen in society and self if God and his ways were primary?

_____

_____

In God's original order, man worked for God and God blessed him—that was the order of the day. This remains the fundamental order of things for God's creation. However, the record of Genesis 3 reminds us that something drastic has happened to this order. While the origin and motivation for work stand, they have been seriously marred by man's decision to be independent and do his own thing. What happened? God's judgment. To pretend there can be a Utopian society or complete self-fulfillment without dealing with this radical problem assumes an idealism of the most fantastic proportions. Let's be sure we understand what really happened.

Read Genesis 3:14–19. Having noted before that verse 15 tells of God's gracious plan to redeem his people through "the seed of the woman," in the meantime what specific curse did God pronounce upon

(1) the woman?_____

(2) the man? _____

A study of this portion in its original Hebrew makes clear that the pain of verse 16 and the toil of verse 17 are the same word.

(The King James Version translates both "sorrow.") How does this speak to family unity?

_____

_____

Why do you believe God addressed the curse on childbearing to the woman and the curse on cultivating the field to the man? Weren't these tasks given to both of them in Genesis 1:28?

_____

_____

The normal situation in God's economy both from creation and from the curse points to *her* as the childbearer and homemaker and to *him* as the breadwinner and protector. Would you agree or disagree? (Read Titus 2:3–5 and 1 Timothy 5:8 before you answer.)

_____

_____

_____

_____

A common idea today goes like this: "Work itself is God's curse on man for his sin." But look at Genesis 5:28, 29: was Lamech looking for escape from work or for the lifting of the curse on work when he named his son Noah ("rest")?

_____

_____

While many of the Hebrew words for "work" in the Old Testament include the idea of fatigue, what particular reason did God give his people in Deuteronomy 5:12–15 for work in the six days, but especially for rest on the Sabbath? (You may want to compare this with Exodus 20:8–11.)

How does this idea of being "redeemed" from toil show itself in Jesus' invitation in Matthew 11:28–30?

The very fact that Jesus spoke of our taking up his yoke and his toil reminds us that work is still there; but what difference does Jesus make?

Even though Christians will live and work in a world under God's curse until the final resurrection as indicated by Romans 8:18–25, how does Paul encourage Christians in 1 Corinthians 15:58 to do their work while they wait?

77

Summary

We should view work from the standpoint of three important trusts. First, man as one flesh received from God the mandate to work. It is, after all, his creation and we are accountable to him. Second, because of man's rebellion against God both male and female have suffered the curse of God that brought sorrow to their work—both to childbearing and to cultivating the earth. Whether man does his work for God or not, he cannot escape the results of this curse. Economic idealists who believe their systems will work but refuse to face up to the fundamental condition of man's sinfulness as whistling in the dark. However, the good news of God's grace promises rest in the seed of the woman. In Jesus Christ we find what some have called "substantial healing," and in him we can work with a great measure of hope and joy. So, our model family works; and because they are given to walking in his ways, God blesses them with contentment.

Walking in His Ways

1. Materialism has become a way of life in many parts of the world. Religiously speaking, do you see any fundamental difference between Marxist materialism and capitalistic materialism?

2. Of the following approaches to life work, which would you think a Christian family should teach their children?

☐ You should plan to do what your parents have done.
☐ You should seek work which provides the most bene-
  fits.
☐ If you want to serve God, you should be a minister.
☐ What do you like to do? You should do that.
☐ You should keep asking God to show you throughout
  life.
☐ Other _____

3. In your opinion what would be the effect if Christian families
   in general committed themselves to living on one income,
   and in the main followed the principle of the wife majoring in
   homemaking while the husband brought home the bacon:
   on family life? On the economy?

8

WORK — A TEAM PROJECT

*The wealth of society is created by the workers,
peasants and working intellectuals. If they take their
destiny into their own hands, follow a Marxist-
Leninist line and take an active attitude in solving
problems instead of evading them, there will be no
difficulty in the world which they cannot overcome.*
(Mao Tse-Tung, 1955)

This statement, and many others like it, have motivated one
of the greatest international coalitions ever to be launched. Its
focal point: workers. The battle cry: "Unite!" Hence a great
team effort of world-wide proportions has characterized the
economic and political arena of the twentieth century.

From a Christian point of view, what fundamental error lies
embedded in the above statement?

_____

_____

Suppose we were to change the above statement. In line two
we change the word "peasants" to "middle class." Then let's
alter the volatile term "Marxist-Leninist" label to "capitalistic."
Now could a Christian agree with it? Why or why not?

_____

One of the great tasks of the family that would walk in God's ways must be to teach the next generation how to *think through* the implications of their commitment to Jesus Christ. Otherwise they can easily become "fellow travelers" with all kinds of error. In this section of our study we want to build on chapter 7 and consider how we can develop a Christian lifestyle for our work —and learn it together. How did God warn his people in Deuteronomy 4:9 about this? (See context also.)

_____

_____

_____

_____

A Team Objective

Let's make sure first of all that we have embraced a clear objective for our work as a family. Jesus addresses the subject in the Sermon on the Mount in Matthew 6:19–34.

What root principle, negatively stated, checks our objective in verse 24?

_____

_____

How does verse 21 explain why this is true?

_____

_____

This dual perspective, this idea that we can indeed serve both God and riches, has become the American way of life, the American dream. That is, you *can* have your cake and eat it too. Following the 1929 Depression the objective of many Americans was to regain economic prosperity. They tried to keep God in the picture; but later, when their children saw inconsistency between their profession of faith and their lifestyle and resolved to abandon Jesus and his church, the parents were mystified. Would you side with the parents in this instance or with the children? Why?

_____

_____

In sharp contrast, what objective does Jesus require of his true followers in verse 33?

_____

_____

The hard question we must ask ourselves goes something like this: In spite of what we may say, does our lifestyle teach our children to make their decisions regarding life in general, but work in particular, on the basis of the kingdom of God or on the kingdom of riches? For example:

(1) Why do you live where you live?

_____

_____

(2) Why do you work where you work?

_____

_____

(3) Can you recommend to your children making their decisions about such things on the same basis you have made yours? Explain.

_____

_____

_____

Another reason for the family to keep worship as the top priority comes in right there. If your family gathers together each day to pray for his kingdom to come, for his will to be done *in your family* as it is in heaven, you avoid many powerful temptations.

A Team Plan

Having God's objective for our work leads us to develop a plan of life which expresses that goal. Here's a way we can approach the forming of a united plan. In 1 Timothy 3:1-13 God's word outlines the qualifications for officers in Christ's church.

The church is to be above all the clearest expression of God's kingdom on earth. We observe that qualifications for both offices outlined here include a well-managed family. What reason does Paul give for that here?

_____

_____

Family management in biblical terms involves both unity and structure, as we noticed in chapter 4. Here Paul makes clear that church officers are to be models in themselves so others newer to the faith and less mature can learn how to walk in God's ways. According to 1 Peter 5:3, where Peter also addresses church officers, what means are these officers to use to lead?

_____

_____

What quality is to be exhibited by everyone? (vs. 5)

_____

_____

The family that avoids a power-structure mentality can work together under Christ's lordship, each member filling his role for the good of the whole. In your order of importance, number the following considerations which must be planned.
- ☐ What job father will do and where
- ☐ What kind of education the children will have
- ☐ What responsibilities are hers and what are his
- ☐ What chores the children will do

- ☐ Whether work will be done on the Lord's day or not
- ☐ When meals will be eaten together and at what time
- ☐ When the family will go to bed and get up
- ☐ What decisions require family consensus
- ☐ What will be the ground rules around the house
- ☐ Other _____

Putting things in order like this may seem strange for a culture left to "do your own thing." What would you say children learn about responsibility when such planning and regular review involve them?

_____

_____

Name the side effects for planning their lives when children are routinely taught no one has time for family worship, family meals, family conversation or family projects.

_____

_____

On the other hand, learning to be a family takes a very natural bent when those fundamental principles of biblical planning are employed. We should recognize that the near-panic gripping some households definitely has a solution. However, it will no doubt require what the Bible calls "repentance." Do you have a clear idea of this biblical term? How do you define it?

_____

_____

A Team "Storehouse"

Let's look at one other aspect of family teamwork: finances. In Matthew 6, which we reviewed, Jesus was not condemning the use of finances but their misuse. Rather than be our god, wealth should be our servant for helping us obey God's will. How can that work itself out in a family?

We have already suggested that prayer before meals, plus a time for family worship, lays the groundwork. By our practice we acknowledge that everything we have is a gift from God. How did Jesus stress the "kingdom" view of ownership in Luke 14:33?

_____

_____

The root idea here is stewardship, a term largely displaced in our culture by the idea of private ownership. Private ownership was never intended to mean something is *mine* rather than *yours*. Rather it was to distinguish between my responsibility and the government's. But we have forgotten that everything belongs to Jesus Christ and that we are but stewards of what he gives to our private and collective oversight. Our children tend to be cultured to live out their basic selfishness, which comes built-in from birth and expresses itself in a "Mine!" mentality. We must reckon with this attitude. Instead we must think and plan in terms of God's kingdom. Let's work on some positive approaches.

(1) In Acts 4:32 we find an attitude toward ownership. How could this be implemented as a family? Give one illustration. (See also John 17:9, 10.)

_____

(2) In 2 Thessalonians 3:6–13 what joint responsibility are we to build into our family life? (Review again 1 Timothy 5:8.)

(3) Malachi 3:10 has been well known among God's people. How do we appropriate this principle as a family?

(4) A positive note also sounds out from Ephesians 4:28. What plan could a family use to share its finances?

Summary

Many Christians are today talking "community" in a new way. Individualism and self-seeking, American free enterprise gone astray, are begetting a backlash. Some, overreacting to injustice, will buy the statement by Mao Tse-Tung heading this chapter. But others will defend a capitalistic materialism to the death. Learning to be a family in the twentieth century demands repentance. We must turn around, and we must begin at home.

By committing ourselves to the service of Jesus and his kingdom as our overriding motive, by planning as a family unit, by making decisions on the basis of Christ's word and by adopting a serious stewardship concerning our possessions and wealth as God's people, we can set an example for our generation that really honors God. We must be ready to pay a price when we get serious about living under God in America.

Walking in His Ways

1. After reviewing the two chapters on work, what in particular has God impressed upon you for your family?

_____

_____

2. Someone has suggested that Christian community as a concept comes about as an extension of family unity. Do you agree?

_____

_____

3. How would you respond to a man's turning down a job in order to spend more time with his family, even though he would make less money and would find inferior working conditions?

_____

_____

4. Do you think a wife should take a job just to make more money?

_____

_____

9

RELAXATION —
A CHRISTIAN PERSPECTIVE

We hold these truths to be self-evident; that all men are created equal; that they are endowed by their creator with certain inalienable rights; that among these are life, liberty, and the pursuit of happiness.

By now you have discovered that this study on the family takes seriously those subtle ideas which comprise the thought patterns of a society. In Genesis 3 Satan deceived Eve with an idea growing out of his own rebellious nature. And he has been following the same course of action ever since. To what did the tempter appeal in Genesis 3:4, 5? (Compare verse 6 with 1 John 2:15, 16.)

_____

_____

This quest for personal pleasure, a wry twist on what our Declaration of Independence calls pursuit of happiness, grows out of a heart steeped in self-centeredness. But its philosophical roots arise out of what ancient Greeks called "hedonism," a term that is returning to the American vocabulary. What do you find when you look up "hedonism" in the dictionary?

_____

_____

_____

_____

Before we jump to the conclusion that happiness must be wrong and that the long face is after all the sign of piety, we must remember that our model family of Psalm 128 lives in happiness. However, we may be helped if we analyze the difference between happiness resulting from "walking in his ways" and the happiness pursued by hedonists. Let's contrast these two ways of life.

Not Escape but Reflection

In Psalm 128 happiness follows work. And we have entitled this chapter "Relaxation" rather than "Pleasure," for we should worship and work with pleasure. Relaxation is different. To relax means to loosen—that is, to cease from concentration. Can you see then that relaxation contrasts with and naturally follows work? How does this pattern show itself in Genesis 2:1–3?

_____

_____

When God viewed his work as noted in Genesis 1:31 how did it appear to him?

_____

92

Here then lies a most important truth: When God relaxed from his work he took time to see what he had made. In the same way man is to work and also take time to reflect on what he has done. In order for this to prove most satisfying, what should be true of his work?

Hedonists however lack a correct view of work. They do not work for God and his glory. They work for self-gratification. When work becomes tedious—and because of God's curse it most certainly does—they seek escape. Knowing they have to work to eat they endure the toil, but the pursuit of happiness becomes the thing to do on the weekend. Anything to escape what one does not enjoy doing! Do you believe the desire to have a shorter workweek fits this pattern? Explain.

We have already explained the toil involved in a world under the curse, so we understand the need for rest. But if our children will be delivered from the threat of hedonism the family must take time to reflect on its work. Can you suggest a way to implement this in your family?

Not Fulfillment but Obedience

Psychological hedonism says that people ultimately will just *do* the thing that gives the most pleasure. Perhaps that's another way of saying man's heart has become dominated by selfish desire. Philosophical hedonism, however—sometimes called ethical hedonism—states that people *should* pursue what gives the greatest happiness. In other words, happiness should be man's goal in life. That was John Stuart Mill's view in his writings, which to a large degree have come to be our interpretation of "the pursuit of happiness." Can you name three evidences of this philosophy in our society today?

(1)_____

_____

(2)_____

_____

(3)_____

_____

Suppose, for example, men espouse the "playboy" philosophy—openly committed to hedonism—and begin to exploit women for their own pleasure. How does this necessarily affect society's view of the husband-wife relationship?

_____

_____

_____

_____

Many single people have adopted a "fulfillment" philosophy of life, and it can often be the reason they are afraid to get married. "Would my partner rob me of my fulfillment?" they ask. Many parents have unwittingly taught them this viewpoint by their own lifestyle. If you would recognize hedonism, watch for the "fulfillment"mentality. How does this conflict with the expression in Psalm 128, and throughtout the Bible, "Who walk in his ways"?

_____

_____

We conclude once again that man was not created for fulfillment but for obedience to God. Do you think the family's relaxation should be a matter of obedience? Explain.

_____

_____

Not Indulgence but Refreshment

In James 4:1-4 the Bible gives a convicting commentary on the results of a hedonistic lifestyle. In verses 1 and 3 the actual Greek work "hedonism" is used (translated lusts, pleasures or passions). How would you summarize the results of such a life-style from this passage?

_____

_____

_____

_____

Whether it's drugs, sex, gluttony, retirement or just plain af-fluence, a life built on indulgence leads to anything but true hap-piness. In sharp contrast, what term appears in Exodus 23:12 and Exodus 31:17 describing the true purpose of relaxation?

_____

_____

How often was this opportunity to be provided?

_____

_____

A growing number of employees are today being exploited by their employers under the guise of commercial interest and job security. What happens to the family when a work obsession commands all seven days of the week? Why does it happen?

_____

_____

_____

_____

Not Diversion but Variation

One of the side effects of hedonism is boredom—trying to find something to fill up the time. We see it as an expression of self-centeredness in our children when they say, "There isn't anything to do!" We see it in adults as they search for something to fill up their leisure. Sometimes the problem hits hardest at retirement. How does Isaiah 57:20, 21 describe a wicked person's restlessness?

_____

_____

Relaxation for the family that walks in his ways, on the other hand, expresses itself as variety within God's universe. Can you name seven variations God has built into the universe which by their very nature help dispel boredom through contrast?

(1) _____   (4) _____

(2) _____   (5) _____

(3) _____   (6) _____

(7) _____

How rewarding it becomes when we understand the wonder of God and his creation! What do you think of the young person's remark to the effect that his father was so busy working all his life he never saw the sunset?

_____

_____

Not Originality but Creativity

Where hedonism has become the conscious or unconscious philosophy of life, there you will find much originality. To get rid of the sameness man will try to break out so he can say, "This was *my* idea!" To encourage this, there is money in being different. Much of what has been peddled as "art" has been contaminated by an ego-trip mentality motivated by money. Often it started at home.

While the results of some originality may be true art, what did God see in the imaginations of the human heart when left to itself? See Genesis 6:5.

_____

_____

The authors of this text believe the term "creativity" may best describe how we are to exercise our imaginations under God, avoiding the connotations accompanying originality in a hedonistic culture. What can our children learn from our being a creative family.

_____

_____

Summary

Relaxation therefore, instead of pursuing happiness, rounds out the lifestyle of the family walking in his ways as they worship and work. In it all God bestows blessedness—or God-centered happiness—on those who love and serve him. Hedonism, in sharp contrast, sets pleasure as man's goal. And whether it comes in the small package of self-centeredness or the economy-sized affluent society, the goals and results are the same. It's rightly called the pursuit of happiness, for it can never be caught. Instead, relaxation with reflection, in obedience, for refeshment, as variation and by creativity integrates with a universe centered in the living God. Learning to be a family involves developing this Christian perspective.

Walking in His Ways

1. What significance do you see in God's having described our model family in terms of poetry? What words in the song spark your imagination?

   _____

   _____

2. What does your family enjoy doing together for relaxation? Does it express the five aspects of relaxation in this chapter?

   _____

   _____

3. How would you talk with a young person whose point of reference focused on personal fulfillment?

_____

_____

10

RELAXATION —
"REMEMBER THE SABBATH"

To convert family relaxation from a perspective into a practical program would seem to come next. How can we actually learn to do this as a family? Rather than plunge into that fascinating challenge now, why not put that before your family? Instead of just looking for the easy way—like the hedonist—be creative. Begin to make this a matter of serious prayer in your worship as a family. Review your reasons for work and your work schedules. Then start talking in the family about biblical relaxation.

Remember what we said in the introduction to this section on page 49? "Life in covenant with him is personal and we learn through the process of obedience, actually 'walking' in his ways. He shows us." We believe you can see how this principle applies to many creative things if you will seek to walk obediently. He will show you many new and enjoyable things to do.

This chapter addresses just one aspect of walking in his ways which our culture—and many Christians—have flagrantly disobeyed. To seek to work out techniques for relaxation while at the same time passing by *his* way for relaxation does not make much sense. What fundamental principle does God make clear to his disobedient people in Isaiah 1:19, 20? (You may wish to review the whole chapter.)

_____

_____

_____

A Creation Ordinance

Once again going back to Genesis, we learn from 2:1–3 something fundamental about God's order of things. What is it?

_____

_____

What do you think it means when the Bible says about the seventh day that God

(1) blessed it? _____

(2) sanctified/hallowed it? _____

When God gave his people his law at Mount Sinai as recorded in Exodus 20, what reason did he give in verses 8–11 for

(1) work on six days? _____

(2) rest on the seventh? _____

Here we have a most significant guideline about life in this universe. Passing over the question of the length of the days of creation, God distinctly reveals from his own example a relationship between work and rest. And he roots this relationship in his own example. Why do you suppose this commandment in Exodus 20 begins with the word "Remember?"

_____

_____

A Family Affair

Let's analyze this commandment a bit further. To whom would you say it is addressed in general? In particular? (See Exodus 20:8–11.)

_____

_____

_____

_____

According to the parallel passage in Deuteronomy 5:12–15 who was to benefit from this policy? How?

_____

_____

_____

_____

This change of pace provided by God for his people set them apart—as did the rest of their lifestyle—from the surrounding pagan cultures. But it was far more than "going to church." Notice that it involved all seven days, or what we might call a God-centered attitude toward time and its use. Technology has put timepieces on our wrists, but telling time seems a bit useless if we have no sense of its ultimate value. From the standpoint of logic alone, how could one day out of seven for rest and for remembering God benefit our families?

_____

_____

_____

_____

An Economic Principle

Remembering that the sabbath was instituted at creation before sin entered into the world, we can recognize something of a broad truth running through Scripture. How does Proverbs 10:22 make this clear?

_____

_____

According to Leviticus 26, God's relationship to his people involved both blessing for obedience and cursing for the disregarding of God's word. What did he say about the land in verses 34, 35?

_____

_____

Aware of God's attitude, how did Nehemiah treat those who would have taken over the sabbath for commercial purposes? Look at Nehemiah 13:15–22.

_____

_____

_____

_____

A culture having sold its soul for gain will in the very process rob itself of God's blessing and bring upon itself economic reversals—unless, that is, there are those who understand God's creation ordinances and bear witness by their conduct. Remembering Jesus' teaching that God's purpose for the sabbath never ruled out works of necessity and mercy (see Matthew 12:9–14 as one example), how can your family apply this principle in its work and rest habits?

_____

_____

_____

_____

A Personal Blessing

It's still true: to walk in his ways, even in the matter of relaxation, leads to blessedness and contentment. Why? We live in a personal universe, and he cares.

Some people believe that to set aside the sabbath—now the first day of the week—from the normalcy of the other six days suggests some kind of pharisaical legalism. But that could be said of any law. The solution is not lawlessness, but obedience from a thankful heart. That can only come about through true conversion to faith in Jesus Christ, to an appreciation for the law of God. Read, for example, Isaiah 58:13, 14. What two lifestyles are contrasted here?

_____

_____

_____

_____

What blessing is here attached to a proper response to God's will for the use of the sabbath?

_____

_____

The challenge to Christian families today goes deeper than learning some innovative ways to relax, helpful as those may be. We must first relearn the matter of obedience inside a culture that has to a very great extent thrown out as obsolete the truth of God's sovereignty over time, work and relaxation. We expect that from unbelievers. While God may bring his displeasure down upon *them*, he most surely will withhold his favor from those who have named his name as their God—and yet disobey. We have a great opportunity to see our families prosper by seeking to apply this principle. Have you as a family talked about the principle? The blessing? If not, will you do so now? What key idea would you stress?

_____

_____

A Practical Suggestion

The authors recognize there may be many other questions to be discussed about the sabbath. What is covered here builds on what has generally been considered the teaching of Scripture by the historic Christian church. Care must be observed not to become judgmental toward fellow believers in this matter, for even within the parameters of the broad principle every family must decide on certain ground rules for its own household. Two things seem clear from Scripture in addition to the mandate to work six days: (1) commerce must cease on the Christian sabbath as a general rule among Christians and (2) the worship of God must dominate. How does your family stand in terms of these fundamentals?

_____

_____

Beyond this the authors have been helped in making application by "relaxing" our use of some things like the bicycles, the TV, home repairs and schoolwork. When asked by the children on some occasions, "What's wrong with that?" we have simply replied, "Nothing—but does it help you 'remember'?" By designating these things as ways of showing God we want to remember him we can then make use of any of them when it becomes necessary without confusing the children. Thus the family learns to remember the sabbath. The result? The blessing of God.

Summary

As we obey God, we learn. He shows us. Giving ourselves to serve him rather than our own self-pleasures, we develop a posture of teachability. It's important not to disobey God in the area of relaxation where he has set forth certain fundamentals. "Remember the Sabbath" takes us back to creation and to a recognition of our belonging to God within his universe. We have his pattern for work and relaxation. With the day of rest we are also reminded that Jesus has lifted the curse from those who trust in him. And because of his resurrection Christians largely remember the first day of the week, which in turn points us ahead to our eternal rest with God. So in a real sense each Lord's day refreshes us in these things—and after all, that's the best kind of relaxation. With it, we are ready for next week's work.

Walking in His Ways

1. If you were to analyze your family's approach to the sab-bath, how would you check the items below?
   ☐ We have really never discussed it.
   ☐ We make it special by_____
   ☐ We attend worship services together.
   ☐ We try to make it a time for family togetherness.
   ☐ We have convictions, but we've become careless.
   ☐ Other _____

2. If you have made some effort toward observing the sab-bath as a day of rest, what ground rules have you developed? How did you arrive at them?

_____

_____

3. What do you think Christians should do about the practice of commerce and sports on the Lord's day?

_____

_____

11

MINISTRY — SEEING CHRIST AT WORK

> Behold, how good and how pleasant it is
> For brothers to dwell together in unity!
> It is like the precious oil upon the head,
> Coming down upon the beard,
> Even Aaron's beard,
> Coming down upon the edge of his robes.
> It is like the dew of Hermon,
> Coming down upon the mountains of Zion;
> For there the LORD commanded the blessing —
> life forever.   — Psalm 133

Many persons have attempted to express the marvel of God's blessing, but none have excelled this brief psalm. Found in the same section of the Psalms where we have been viewing a model family, Psalm 133 speaks of unity. It's a fitting place for us to begin this fourth function of family life, for we have throughout this entire study looked at the family as a unit, not as a collection of individuals or a regimen of roles.

Before we get into the matter of ministry, pause long enough to catch the drift of Psalm 133. To picture the pleasantness of the unity described, David the poet uses two illustrations, oil and dew. What quality about each makes his point? (Look at Exodus 30:22–33 for more insight on the oil.)

(1) Oil _____

(2) Dew _____

What symbol do you see in the threefold "coming down" (Ps. 133)?

_____

_____

Obviously the unity described here means more than some cleverly-devised technique. It breathes of a oneness born out of a right relationship to God. In theology we would probably use the term "grace" to qualify it, meaning it is the gift of God. How does the blessing referred to in the last line remind you of Romans 6:23?

_____

_____

Once again we find ourselves reminded of our model family in Psalm 128, for interestingly enough the blessing prayed for in Psalm 128:5 is the same as the blessing of Psalm 133:3. When that blessing comes down from God himself, one evidence of it is unity, and it affects the whole household.

The Meaning of Ministry

Too often we have thought of ministry as something done by a minister. That isn't wrong exactly but it's misleading. Ministry really means service. One has not read his New Testament very far before he encounters Mark 10:45. What model is present there? How?

_____

_____

What brought on this statement by Jesus? Was it unity or disunity? Mark 10:35–44.

_____

_____

To minister together as a family, a church, a business or a school requires a "servant attitude" which affects everything and everyone. It brings with it an atmosphere such as we find in Psalm 133. So in a real sense, when the family learns to minister in unity it has begun to learn how to function as a servant to all. This must not be limited to the sabbath nor to the church: we should do our work, as well as our worship and relaxation, as Christ's servants. How would such an attitude help

(1) an employer? _____

(2) an employee? _____

(3) a husband? _____

(4) a wife? _____

(5) children? _____

The Source of Ministry

While ministry flows from a servant attitude, the service itself must be considered separately. Some persons have developed in their minds a category of things which they would call "service." They are often things they would call "spiritual" or religious. But we have already learned that *everything* is religious. Service is like that. How does Romans 12:1, 2 integrate our concept of service?

_____

_____

According to Ephesians 2:10 why is it, after all, that Christians serve God?

_____

_____

Our walking in his ways—in other words, in good works or service—speaks a clear language proclaiming that God has come down upon us with his blessing in Christ. Our service does not flow from a self-imposed discipline but from a God-disposed attitude. How does this tie in with the same truth expressed in Colossians 2:6, 7? What is the significance of the term "in him"?

_____

_____

_____

114

When our family begins to recognize more and more of what it means to be in Christ, ministry or service will surely follow. It will come from God. It will produce a wonderful unity within the household because it is based on our union with Christ. Whatever may befall that home—and God often brings suffering into Christian homes—a tremendous resource of strength will be evident. How does Paul testify to this truth in a personal way in 2 Corinthians 12:9, 10?

Ministry therefore becomes the reality of God's working out his purposes for us. When such blessing comes down upon a family is it any wonder that they prosper as found in Psalm 128:5? How does John 15:5 emphasize the same point?

The Secret of Ministry

Actually there's no secret to it at all—it just seems that way. So few people, families included, seem to recognize our union with Christ as the means by which Christians are to live. To be sure, there is a mystery to it all. Theologians have adopted terms to cover it. They call it our "mystical union with Christ." That is not "mysticism," like the Eastern religions. (If you don't know that term look it up in a dictionary.) When Jesus Christ sent his

Spirit into his people on the Day of Pentecost it was—
and is—as though Jesus himself came to live in us. How do the
following passages show this to be true?

(1) John 14:23 _____

(2) 1 Corinthians 6:14–20_____

(3) Romans 8:9–11 _____

Even though the apostle Paul claims to have extended himself to his limits, in the final analysis how did he accomplish his
service? Look at his comment in 1 Corinthians 15:10.

_____

_____

Why do you suppose he told Timothy what he did in 2 Timothy 2:1?

_____

_____

The secret of ministry, if there is a secret, means simply that
we draw upon the life of Christ by his Spirit in us to perform
what we are to perform. As a family, we look to him to put
within us by his Holy Spirit what we ourselves do not possess.
By their union with Christ God's people inherit not just Christ's
resources but Christ himself. How does Ephesians 6:10 teach
this?

_____

_____

_____

_____

When a family gives itself to walking in his ways and learns how to cultivate its union with Christ through worship, work and relaxation, they begin to see that union binding them together in one spirit. They begin to experience the reality of Galatians 5:22, 23 in their relationships, and the oneness first described in Genesis 2:24 permeates their family life. It's not a dream world—Christ is present, and he brings the unity which parallels the oil and dew of Psalm 133. According to 2 Corinthians 2:14 how did that mean ministry for the apostle Paul? (See the context also.)

_____

_____

_____

_____

Summary

Ministry means service and therefore must flow from the heart of a servant. Our perfect model for such service is the Lord Jesus Christ himself, who not only demonstrated what it means to lay down one's life for another's need but also by his Spirit actually empowers his people to live the same way. While we do not atone for other people's sins—we don't need to since he did

117

—we do indeed live out every part of our lives through our union with him. It is therefore Christ in us who gives us the ability to give ourselves to serving one another. Unity in the family must be cultivated—in our work, in our relaxation, in our worship. Since all Christians are called to be his servants, all of our life is to be service. And it is mystically—yet truly—accomplished as he blesses us, and only so. Such blessing is to mark all we do. That is the reason we pray for it and daily seek it from him.

Walking in His Ways

1. What part of this particular chapter do you find

   most difficult? _____

   most helpful? _____

2. Why do you think people tend to think of ministry as having to do only with church rather than with our everyday work as well?

   _____

   _____

3. Twentieth-century culture has seen a growing attitude which tends to look down on the woman for whom homemaking is a vocation. How does that attitude compare to the servant attitude described in this chapter?

   _____

   _____

4. Suppose a family has a child whose mental or physical capacities are in some way abnormal. How does Christ's call to minister as a family become a blessing in such a situation to the parents? To the children? To the handicapped?

_____

_____

5. As you reread Psalm 128:5 and compare it with Psalm 106:4 and 5, would you say that you as a family are experiencing what is prayed for there? Have you been praying for it as a family?

_____

12

MINISTRY —
A HOUSE BY THE SIDE OF THE ROAD

Let me live in a house by the side of the road
And be a friend to man.

Although Sam Walter Foss did not say so in his poem, the lines suggest that there probably would have been a front porch on his house by the side of the road. American homes, reflecting introverted Americans, no longer bid the passers-by to come and sit. Instead of the porch it's the patio—in the back—often with a fence to block visibility.

But it's still a house, and that's important. The authors will never forget having watched Cyprus refugees seeking shelter after having had to flee their homes during the Turkish invasion. Most were unable to return, so their countrymen opened their homes. This was ministry!

Let's take a look at the possibilities of using our homes for such service. Building on the truths in the previous chapter, we recall at the outset that true ministry derives from Christ himself, not from the house. If we hope to see God using our house, certainly we must also dedicate it to God's service. For some people that will be very difficult. Self-centeredness and self-fulfillment may in our culture be most deeply imbedded in our attachment to our houses. How did wealthy Abraham live according to Hebrews 11:8–10?

_____

_____

Family ministry may take many forms, but the possibilities of a united ministry through the home itself develops most naturally. While we expect Christ to perform his ministry through us, our conscious obedience is necessary as well.

Location

Our model family of Psalm 128 does have a house, but we are not told where it was located. What do you believe are the governing influences which determine where people in your own circle of friends live?

_____

_____

In spite of the fact that much of the nation lives on wheels, experience shows that where we live affects ministry in at least three directions:

(1) Toward the people of God. For example, how close are you to other members of your church (distance, not time)?

_____

_____

(2) Toward your neighbors. The word "neighbor" comes from an Anglo-Saxon expression meaning "near dweller." Do

you intend to minister only to people living close to you when we know that Jesus reminded us to love our neighbors as ourselves? How?

_____

_____

(3) Toward your community. Every dwelling belongs to a particular civic district. What natural ministry follows for those who are serious citizens?

_____

_____

The reason we put the above directions in this order is that, before we can really decide where we will live, we must choose our people. Our model family, you remember, maintained a solid relationship to Jerusalem, the city of God. What decision did Moses have to make about his people? See Hebrews 11:24–26.

_____

_____

Even though we expect ministry to flow from our relationship with Christ—and his with us—and even though God is our dwelling place as Moses said in Psalm 90, we expect our ministry to be inseparably linked with our geographical location. Where we have a choice in the matter—and under God we do—we should do so in terms of these considerations. We can, after all, live "by the side of the road."

Appearance

Since God has created such a beautiful world, as photographs from outer space have revealed, we must not consider beauty as unimportant. What beautiful description does the psalmist give us of the inside of the house in Psalm 128?

_____

_____

A house need not be expensive or elaborate to be good to behold. Below are some qualities which do not cost money but which do minister to a community. If you want to live by the side of the road and be a friend to man, you should consider them.

(1) *Pleasant*—Every house can show some quality of the Creator's beauty. For example, people in Ireland like roses in their front gardens. Where garden space is unavailable, there can be window boxes. Is there one feature about your home that ministers beauty to the passers-by?

_____

_____

(2) *Clean*—No, "cleanliness is next to godliness" does not appear in Scripture. But certainly one can reason a connection between cleansing from sin and an orderly lifestyle. When people look at your home, do they see that it's clean?

_____

_____

(3) *Modest*—In 1 Timothy 2:9 Paul commands women to dress modestly (which does not necessarily mean drably). How might a modest home reflect this principle?

_____

_____

(4) *Open* — There must be something better than "KEEP OFF THE GRASS." In Greek culture the doors of the houses summoned your attention. It's by design, for an attractive door bids welcome. Is there something about *your* home which mutely says, "We are your friends?"

_____

_____

We must be careful here. Some people treat their houses as some sort of show place—everything must be for looks. But the house by the side of the road has a particular attractiveness which communicates love and compassion. Everything should be for ministry.

Vocation

The lifestyle of a family communicates its sense of calling. That's the meaning of vocation, a "calling." The family's vocation may have a bearing on where it locates, but it is the family's commitment to share the home's comforts and joys that determines the scope of its ministry. Here are some ways it happens; write down the applications.

(1) Romans 12:13 _____

(2) Matthew 25:35, 36 _____

(3) Philemon 1–7 _____

Let's get even more practical. If you called on the family in Psalm 128, do you believe there would be someone home when you knocked? Why?

_____

_____

To what extent do you believe a family's need to have someone available in the home should influence

(1) the husband's type of work? _____

(2) the wife's holding an outside job? _____

How do you believe Matthew 25:41–46 should be interpreted in terms of family ministry?

_____

_____

It has become evident in many neighborhoods that, while the houses may be by the side of the road, they are empty. When someone seriously inquires about a ministry for women in the church they should be reminded of the church's ministry through the home. In a society where homes are crumbling, an inhabited and ministering house has unlimited opportunities.

Vision

Every household committed to seek first the kingdom of God will see itself in a larger context than its own neighborhood. While maintaining a primary concern for its own community, it keeps the world picture in view as well. This perspective may not be evident on the outside, but those living and visiting on the inside will find the "Kingdom vision" as the dominant theme:

(1) In the conversation. Which of the following would most color your talk as a family in terms of Christ's kingdom?

☐ Newscasts   ☐ Letters   ☐ Church activities
☐ Sermons   ☐ Conversions   ☐ Accidents/sickness
☐ Scripture   ☐ Prayer answers   ☐ Other _____

(2) In entertaining guests. How many of the following are a part of your family's regular habit of ministry?

☐ Dinner guests   ☐ Babysitters   ☐ Internationals
☐ Foster children   ☐ Live-ins   ☐ Missionaries

(3) In particular service. Many families have members serving on various committees or in programs designed to meet kingdom needs. In how many of these is your family involved? Explain.

_____

_____

_____

_____

Sometimes these activities can become too heavy and numerous for the full blessing of God. They become counterproductive. Activism can be as destructive to family life as self-preoccupation, so checks and balances are needed. Do you suppose this could be one reason why God appointed shepherds to oversee his flock?

Summary

Houses are where we live, and that makes them important. What happens in the houses depends upon our relationship to Jesus Christ. When we are walking in his ways we will find him directing us into avenues of ministry. After all, *he* came to minister, and all his ways are ministry. Where we live, our home's appearance, how we respond to need, our general commitment to his worldwide kingdom—all begin to show his influence. Mysteriously, the family caught up together in the ministry of Christ finds the children also falling in step. It's not automatic—often there are struggles. But Christ wins. Then come the grandchildren as each generation produces the next. How glorious to see his kingdom coming through the descendants of model families!

Walking in His Ways

1. Have you as a family dedicated your house to the service of Christ? If not, will you do so now?

   _____

2. To what extent do you believe the increase in ministry through our homes could decrease the necessity for so many organized church programs?

_____

_____

3. Have you the time to minister through your home? Explain.

_____

_____

4. Have you ever had the officers of your church visit your home and discuss with you the ministry Christ desires through your household?

_____

5. In what ways have your children been learning ministry through your family life?

_____

_____

CONCLUSION

Learning to be a family in the twentieth century may seem to be too much to expect. After all, many households don't last that long. But this spirit of pessimism is not born of faith: it stems from exactly the opposite—unbelief.

As believers in the living God we have a radically different mentality toward life in general and toward the family in particular. The family was God's idea and he will see to it that families continue. But those that do must walk in his ways. They must fear God and keep his commandments, as Scripture says.

Our study was intended to encourage just that. We have gone back to the foundations which God established and have analyzed the functions of family life in terms of broad categories and the purposes which God himself ordained. We have intentionally avoided the details of technique and problem solving. People can learn to develop techniques by experiment and observation, but they cannot walk in his ways without biblical truth. Life according to that truth is to be lived in Christ as a response of obedience—a conscious and deliberate choosing to do what God says. That's the way we show him our love. We are in covenant with him.

One final word which leads us to think of the family of the future has to do with the family's relationship to the Christian community. Learning to be a family by walking in his ways establishes the foundation for Christian community. We learn "community" at home. In that sense our homes hold the key to the growth of the church. In like fashion, no attempt to be a family will reach success without the input of God's people. Families need the encouragement and support of the church, which means that learning to be a family leads to learning to be a people. Twentieth-century Christians must learn again to act as the people of God in the world. As a world-wide family of sinners redeemed by the blood of Christ we stand united in him, and look for the hearts of our children to be fired by the vision of the kingdom of God!

"Peace be upon Israel!"